TRAVEL WITH THE GREAT EXPLORERS

Explore with

John Cabot

Cynthia O'Brien

Crabtree Publishing Company

www.crabtreebooks.com

Crabtree Publishing Company
www.crabtreebooks.com

Author: Cynthia O'Brien
**Publishing plan research
 and development:** Reagan Miller
Managing Editor: Tim Cooke
Designer: Lynne Lennon
Picture Manager: Sophie Mortimer
Design Manager: Keith Davis
Editorial Director: Lindsey Lowe
Editor: Kelly Spence
Proof reader: Crystal Sikkens
Children's Publisher: Anne O'Daly
**Production coordinator
 and prepress technician:** Tammy McGarr
Print coordinator: Margaret Amy Salter

Produced by Brown Bear Books for
Crabtree Publishing Company

Photographs:
Front Cover: Dreamstime: Norman Pogson cr; Robert Hunt Library: main; Shutterstock: ANCH br; Thinkstock: istock tr.

Interior: Accademia of Venice: 4–5b; Alamy: BrazilPhotos.com 21br, Itsik Marom 13b; Biblioteca Estense Universitaria, Modena: 25c; Bridgeman Art Library: 25t; Bristol Records Office: 5br; Getty Images: Clive Mason/Allsport 12; Gustino Menescardi 28; istockphoto: 24t; Kunsthalle Hamburg: 6b; Marinum Maritme Museum: 14bl; Naval Museum of Madrid: 29t; Princeton Education: 6tl; Robert Hunt Library: 11b, 11br; Philip Henry Gosse 20br; Royal Ontario Museum: 21t; Shutterstock: 16l, 17tc, 22t, Bob Cheung 27b, Everett Historical 5t, Eric Isselée 16c,Igor Kovalchuk 14–15t, David P. Lewis 19t, V. J. Matthew 18b, Brian Maudsley 15c, Morphart Creation 23b, Denis Natal 16r, Paul Paladin 15b, Norman Pogson 19b; Thinkstock: George Burba 7b, istock 13t, 26t, Photodisc 14tr, Photos.com 11t; Topfoto: British Library Board 20, 24b, 26–27, The Granger Collection 7t, 18t, 23t, Ann Ronan Picture Library 10, Smith 17b, World History Archive 4t; University of Idaho: Chris Schnepf 22bl; WordPress: D. C. Bellows 29b.
All other artwork and maps, Brown Bear Books.

Brown Bear Books has made every attempt to contact the copyright holder. If you have any information please contact licensing@brownbearbooks.co.uk

Library and Archives Canada Cataloguing in Publication

O'Brien, Cynthia (Cynthia J.), author
       Explore with John Cabot / Cynthia O'Brien.

(Travel with the great explorers)
Includes index.
Issued in print and electronic formats.
ISBN 978-0-7787-1702-7 (bound).--
ISBN 978-0-7787-1706-5 (paperback).--
ISBN 978-1-4271-7710-0 (pdf).--ISBN 978-1-4271-7702-5 (html)

       1. Cabot, John, -1498?--Juvenile literature. 2. Canada--Discovery and exploration--British--Juvenile literature. 3. Explorers--Great Britain--Biography--Juvenile literature. 4. Explorers--Canada--Biography--Juvenile literature. I. Title. II. Series: Travel with the great explorers

FC301.C3O37 2015   j971.01'14092   C2015-903206-7
                                                                                    C2015-903207-5

Library of Congress Cataloging-in-Publication Data

CIP available at the Library of Congress

Crabtree Publishing Company
www.crabtreebooks.com   1-800-387-7650

Printed in Canada/082015/BF20150630

Published in Canada
Crabtree Publishing
616 Welland Ave.
St. Catharines, ON
L2M 5V6

Published in the United States
Crabtree Publishing
PMB 59051
350 Fifth Avenue, 59th Floor
New York, New York 10118

Published in the United Kingdom
Crabtree Publishing
Maritime House
Basin Road North, Hove
BN41 1WR

Published in Australia
Crabtree Publishing
3 Charles Street
Coburg North
VIC, 3058

CONTENTS

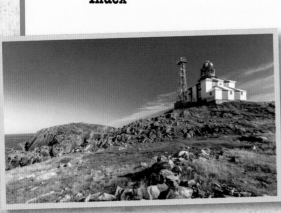

Meet the Boss

John Cabot was the first European to lay claim to the vast continent of North America. His voyages of discovery marked the beginning of Britain's expansion into the New World.

ON THE MOVE

+ Italian has international life

The early life of John Cabot, or Giovanni Caboto, is a mystery. Many historians believe he was born in Genoa, Italy, around 1450. The Caboto family moved to Venice, and Giovanni became a Venetian citizen in 1476. He married his wife Mattea around 1482, and the couple had three sons named Ludovico, Sebastian, and Sancto. By about 1495, the family had moved to Bristol, a bustling English **port**. Caboto's name then became John Cabot in English.

TRADING PLACES

★ **Cabot learns his craft**

During the 1400s, Venice was a busy port of trade between Europe and Asia. Cabot worked as a merchant selling spices, and is believed to have visited the exotic cities of Mecca in Arabia and Alexandria in Egypt. During this time, Cabot learned how to sail ships. He became a master **mariner**, meaning he knew how to **navigate** and captain a vessel.

★ Imagine you are Cabot and you are trying to raise funds for an expedition across the Atlantic. What reasons might you give to get a monarch to support you?

Did you know?

The Italian name *Caboto* translates to "a coastal seaman." This was a common name given to sailors in Italy during the 1400s.

MEETING OF MINDS

☛ Did Cabot meet Columbus?

In the early 1490s, records show that a harbor designer named Johan Caboto Montecalunya worked in Valencia, Spain. This may have been Cabot, using the skills he had learned as a navigator. If so, Cabot might have met Christopher Columbus (above) in Valencia in 1493. Columbus had just discovered the Americas, or the New World, on behalf of Spain. Meeting Columbus may have inspired Cabot to set sail to explore North America himself.

HENRY SAYS YES

+ English king backs Cabot's quest

Cabot asked the rulers of Spain and Portugal to fund an expedition to North America. When they refused, he moved to Bristol in England (right). The English king, Henry VII, agreed to finance Cabot's expedition. He gave Cabot and his sons **letters patent**. These documents gave the Cabots the right to seek a westward route across the Atlantic to Asia—claiming any new lands for England along the way.

Where Are We Heading?

YUCK!

Spices were popular in Europe because food was often old or rotten. Spices helped to mask the bad taste. They also made boring foods more tasty.

John Cabot made two voyages across the Atlantic. He hoped to discover the Northwest Passage—a sea route to East Asia, which had many valuable goods for trading. Cabot failed to find the passage, but discovered a "New-Found-Land" instead.

SPICE IT UP

- ☛ Competition is fierce!
- ☛ Europe can't get enough

Some of the most valuable goods from Asia included spices such as cinnamon, cloves, and nutmeg. It took a long time to transport goods from the Spice Islands of Indonesia (left). Traders had to cross deserts and mountains to reach Europe. Many explorers set out to find a sea route by sailing west across the Atlantic.

EAST IS WEST

- ★ Is this the way to Asia?
- ★ Ice ahead!

In 1492, Italian explorer Christopher Columbus believed he had found Asia when he landed in the Caribbean. Cabot believed finding the Northwest Passage would provide a much quicker way to reach East Asia. This northern route, however, would lie through the dangerous frozen seas of the north (right).

PLENTY OF FISH IN THE SEA

★ **Bucketloads of cod**

Cabot set sail from Bristol on a small ship in May 1497, sailing west past Ireland and out into the Atlantic. Even before he found land, he made an important discovery. The Grand Banks, in the Atlantic Ocean off Newfoundland, are part of North America's **continental shelf**. Conditions there are ideal for fish, especially cod. After Cabot's discovery, the Grand Banks became one of the world's most important fisheries. Fishing boats flocked there from western Europe.

Did you know?

When Europeans settled in Newfoundland, their economy was based on cod from the Grand Banks. The fish were dried or salted and shipped to Europe for food.

NEW-FOUND-LAND

+ Where did Cabot land?

About 35 days after leaving Bristol, Cabot reached land. On June 24, 1497, he landed somewhere on the east coast of Canada. There are several possible locations for his landing, including Labrador, Newfoundland, Cape Breton Island, or mainland Nova Scotia. No one knows the exact location. Cabot claimed the new land for King Henry VII. Cabot believed he had arrived on the northeast coast of Asia, and he named the territory "New-Found-Land."

> **All along the coast they found many fish like those which in Iceland are dried in the open."**
> *John Day reports Cabot's findings in Newfoundland*

JOHN CABOT'S VOYAGE ACROSS THE ATLANTIC

Few details are known about Cabot's voyage to Newfoundland in 1497. Nothing is known about his second voyage. Experts believe he came ashore at one of several possible sites in what is now northeastern Canada.

Labrador

If Cabot sailed west from northwest Ireland, he may have landed near Cape St. Lewis in what is now Labrador. Some experts believe his ship, the *Matthew*, would have been pushed on this northern course by strong currents in the Atlantic Ocean.

Grates Cove

Nova Scotia

Cape Breton

Newfoundland

There are two possible landing sites on Newfoundland: Cape Bauld in the north or Cape Bonavista, to the south. Cabot also may have sailed into the Gulf of St. Lawrence, or he may even have sailed around the whole island of Newfoundland.

Nova Scotia

A more southerly route across the Atlantic may have brought Cabot to land around the present-day site of Halifax, Nova Scotia, from where he may have sailed back along the coasts of Cape Breton Island and Newfoundland.

Cape Breton

Cabot may have landed here on Cape Breton Island, then headed southwest along the coast of Nova Scotia.

Grates Cove

A rock carved with Cabot's name and the names of some of his crew was said to stand in Grates Cove in eastern Newfoundland. The rock has disappeared, but some people believe it had been carved by survivors after Cabot and the others died in a shipwreck on his second voyage in 1498.

Bristol

The only location we know about for sure on Cabot's journey is Bristol, England, where the voyage began and ended.

Scale | 300 miles / 500 km

Bristol

Key

- - - → Cabot's possible route, 1497

Grand Banks

These rich fishing grounds off the coast of Newfoundland may already have been visited by European fishermen before Cabot arrived. His description of the huge numbers of cod there made the Grand Banks a major fishing ground for centuries.

Locator map

Meet the Crew

John Cabot made his journeys on behalf of the English King Henry VII. His crew was mainly made up of English sailors, and may have included one or more of Cabot's own sons.

Clean Shave

Cabot may have taken a barber on his voyage because the fashion at the time was for men not to have beards. More likely, the barber also served as the ship's surgeon.

WHO'S ON BOARD?

★ **18 men set sail on tiny ship**

★ **Crew includes Bristol sailors**

Cabot set sail from Bristol on the *Matthew* (above), a small sailing ship, in May 1497. Most of his crew were English. Also on board were an Italian barber, a cook, a carpenter, and possibly Cabot's son, Sebastian. A priest named Giovanni de Carbonariis later traveled on Cabot's 1498 expedition to North America. He may have set up a church in Newfoundland, but **archaeologists** are still searching for evidence.

THE SPY

+ **Englishman leaks information to Spain**

In 1956, researchers discovered a letter from an English merchant named John Day to the "Lord Grand Admiral." The letter described Cabot's 1497 voyage in great detail. Historians believe Day's real name was Hugh Say, and that the "Lord Grand Admiral" was Christopher Columbus. Say was spying for Columbus! Details of Cabot's voyage may have helped Columbus on his third voyage to the Americas in 1498.

ENGLAND ENTERS THE RACE!

+ Henry VII seeks new routes east

Cabot moved to England with the goal of getting King Henry VII (right) to fund his expedition across the Atlantic. The king knew that Spain and Portugal were also looking for routes to Asia to control the valuable market in spices. Henry wanted to beat them to it. He gave Cabot official permission to set out to discover new lands that were not yet known to Europeans.

KEEPING IT IN THE FAMILY

☛ Explorer's son seeks fortune

Confusion surrounds the story of John Cabot's son, Sebastian. Sebastian told different stories about his life—even claiming some of his father's discoveries as his own. Sebastian said he traveled with his father on the *Matthew*. He also claimed that he had sailed himself to search for the Northwest Passage in 1508.

THE ITALIANS

★ Letters describe Cabot voyage

★ Success—word spreads!

Although Cabot did not leave any logs or journals, other people wrote down his findings. They included two Italians living in London. A Venetian merchant, Lorenzo Pasqualigo, wrote to his brothers about a "Venetian of ours who … discovered mainland 700 leagues away." Meanwhile, an Italian ambassador, Raimondo di Soncino, wrote in a letter that Cabot had "found two new very large and fertile islands."

Check Out the Ride

John Cabot took just one ship on his first voyage across the Atlantic in 1497. The *Matthew* was well suited to the demands of crossing the Atlantic Ocean.

Did you know?

A replica of the *Matthew* was built in Bristol in 1996. In 1997, the replica sailed to Canada to mark the 500th anniversary of Cabot's voyage.

THE *MATTHEW*

+ Sturdy ship for historic voyage

+ Sails suit all conditions

The *Matthew*, which may have been named after Cabot's wife, Mattea, was a small ship similar to the Spanish **caravels** used by Christopher Columbus. The *Matthew* was a three-masted ship that could carry about 50 tons (45 metric tons) of cargo, or goods. The two front masts had square sails to help the ship travel forward. A square or triangular **lateen** sail may have been rigged to the rear mast. Triangular lateen sails were not usually sturdy enough for ocean sailing. Sailors may have used a square sail instead, or different sails depending on the weather.

 Weather Forecast

HEAD WINDS

Winds in the North Atlantic blow mainly from west to east. They average about 16 miles per hour (25.7 km/h). It can be difficult to sail west into a steady wind. Cabot may have used a lateen sail, or may have traveled north or south to find more favorable winds.

SMALL BUT STURDY

★ Strong English oak used for Cabot's ship

The *Matthew* was about 60 feet (18 m) long. It was made from oak. English shipbuilders preferred to use oak to build ships' **hulls** because it was a strong, hard wood. Straight fir trees were used for the tall masts. The *Matthew* was light and fast. It took Cabot 35 days to sail westward into the wind across the Atlantic. On its return voyage, the *Matthew* took just 15 days to reach England in August 1497.

MIND THE GAP

☞ Sealing the ship

Once the ship's hull was ready, builders **caulked** the seams, or gaps, between the planks. This made the ship watertight. Workers hammered **oakum** into the seams and covered them with tar. Once the ship was in the water, the oakum swelled and protected the ship from leaks.

LET'S GO AGAIN

★ King gives Cabot more ships

In 1498, Cabot arranged to make another journey across the ocean. This time Henry VII granted him five ships. In total, Cabot had about 200 crew and enough **provisions** for a year. A storm damaged one of the ships, which returned to Ireland. The others sailed westward, never to be seen again.

Solve It With Science

How Far?

Sailors used the stars or the Sun to work out how far north or south they were. It was much more difficult to figure out how far east or west they had traveled.

According to his fellow sailors, Cabot was a skilled mariner. By 1497, he was an experienced captain who was ready to use all his skills on his voyage to find the Northwest Passage.

SANDS OF TIME

- Grains of sand count the hours
- Course plotted on board

Cabot used **dead reckoning** to estimate the ship's speed and direction. This process relied on two instruments: the sand-glass (right) and the traverse board (left). Each time the sand-glass was turned, a peg was placed in the **compass rose** of the traverse board to track the ship's direction. Pegs were also placed in holes at the bottom of the board to record the ship's speed.

BY THE BOOK

★ Vital facts contained in sailors' logs

Early sailors did not have maps and charts, so **rutters** were used. These were small books in which navigators noted details such as tide times, changes in **currents**, and distances between ports. Cabot would have studied the rutters of Bristol sailors to help him navigate the Atlantic Ocean.

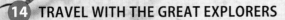

CHECK OUT THE ANGLE

★ **Measuring with stars**

★ **Darkness throws light on position!**

Cabot used an **astrolabe** to show his location at sea. This round, brass instrument had degrees marked on its edge and a moving inner disk. The navigator measured the angle between the horizon and **Polaris**, or the North Star. This calculation gave him an estimate of his **latitude**.

> He started from Bristol, passed Ireland, then bore toward the north in order to sail to the east."
> *John Day describes Cabot's route*

POINT THE WAY

+ Explorer to take scientific log

From the 12th century, European sailors used a compass for direction. A **gimbal** supported the compass and held it upright, even in stormy seas. The compass was marked with 32 points for wind directions, including four main points showing north, south, east, and west. The magnetized needle pointed roughly north. However, it did not account for the differences in Earth's **magnetic field**, so it was not entirely accurate.

TRAVEL UPDATE

Heading West

★ Travelers crossing the Atlantic may be in for a longer journey than they think. Christopher Columbus claimed to have reached the East Indies in Asia and Cabot believed he had reached Cathay, or China. But some people believed Earth was much bigger than Columbus and Cabot thought. Therefore, sailing west to Asia would take much longer.

Hanging at Home

The journey onboard the *Matthew* was tough for the crew. Because the ship was so small, it only carried 18 men. That was not enough to do all the heavy work required to man the vessel.

ALL ABOARD

- ☞ **Explorer stocks up for voyage**
- ☞ **Crew to get beer rations!**

Cabot made sure that the *Matthew* carried enough food for six months. In addition, the crew had a three month supply of water and a gallon of beer a day for each man. Meals consisted of bread (made onboard), salt meat, or smoked fish. Live animals, such as a cow and goats, provided milk. Chickens provided eggs. Eventually, these animals would become fresh meat for the crew.

CASA DI CABOTO

- ★ **The Cabots find a home**
- ★ **Pioneering voyage pays handsomely!**

Cabot was not wealthy when he moved to Bristol, but he had enough money to rent a house. Records show that he lived with his family in a respectable part of town. After his first voyage in 1497, the king gave Cabot £10. This would have been two years pay for an ordinary, working man. In addition, Cabot was given a **pension** of £20 per year.

WATCH OUT FOR WORMS!

★ **Insects breed in ship's flour stores**

★ **Moldy meat on the menu**

The small supply of fresh meat on a ship was not always appetizing. Sailors found maggots and worms in their rations. As a result, most men had worms in their intestines. Other insects also multiplied in food. Weevils crawled into the barrels of flour and bred there. Yuck!

JUST THE CLOTHES ON THEIR BACKS

☛ **Sailors pack light**

Regular seamen were very poor and had few possessions. They usually set sail in the clothes they wore: a linen shirt, a pair of pants, and a woolen coat. They worked barefoot on the wet, slippery deck because it gave them a better grip. They kept their simple leather shoes for wearing on land. None of the clothing they had provided much protection from the cold, wet weather in the Atlantic.

TIME FOR BED

+ No comfort for crew

As the captain, Cabot had a small cabin on the *Matthew*. The rest of the crew slept on deck with only a blanket for warmth. But this was still preferable to sleeping below deck with the cargo and the rats. The crew only slept in this small, cramped, airless space when bad weather forced them to take cover.

Where Do We Land?

When Cabot reached land, he put up a cross, a flag for King Henry VII, and a flag for Pope Alexander VI. Exactly where this happened remains a mystery.

LANDFALL IN LABRADOR?

☞ Did Cabot stay north?

After leaving Bristol, Cabot likely headed to northwest Ireland. If Cabot then traveled due west, he would have made **landfall** on the coast of Labrador, around Cape St. Lewis. From there, Cabot could have explored south along the coast and into the Gulf of St. Lawrence.

OH HAPPY SIGHT!

★ Landfall on the Cape?

★ 500th anniversary celebrated

Legend says that Cabot exclaimed, "O buona vista!" ("O, happy sight!") when he saw Newfoundland. This spot is now called Cape Bonavista. This landing site makes sense if the *Matthew* sailed west and then south due to storms and currents. In 1997, the town of Bonavista celebrated the 500th anniversary of Cabot's landfall in Canada.

THE OTHER ISLAND

According to Soncino's letters, Cabot sailed for some time before arriving at a mainland. If Cabot did sail south from Newfoundland, it is possible that he landed on Cape Breton Island. This small island, part of Nova Scotia, could be one of the two islands Soncino wrote about in his letter. Today, the Cabot Trail, a highway that runs along the coast, honors the explorer's name.

> **Most of the land was discovered after turning back."**
> *John Day's account, which supports a landfall in Newfoundland*

My Explorer Journal

★ **Imagine you lived in one of the places Cabot may have landed. What would some advantages be for your community if you were able to prove Cabot landed there?**

EXPLORER REMEMBERED

☞ **Monuments to Cabot**

☞ **Everyone claims great sailor**

A number of communities have built monuments to support their claim as Cabot's landing site. Cape Bonavista has a statue of Cabot, as does St. John's in Newfoundland. St. John's also has a tower named after Cabot at the top of Signal Hill.

Meeting and Greeting

Cabot did not report seeing any native people when he went ashore in 1497. Instead, he spotted clues that humans lived there. These people were the Beothuk, the aboriginals of Newfoundland.

WHERE IS EVERYONE?

- ☛ Cabot explores inland
- ☛ Explorers find remains of a camp

Although Newfoundland seemed deserted, Cabot's men spotted signs of life. They found a trail that led to the remains of a fire. Nearby was manure, which they guessed came from farm animals. There was also a stick that was carved into points at both ends and painted red. The Beothuk who lived in the area stayed hidden. Cabot had few men and they did not want to risk an encounter with hostile natives.

EXINCTION

+ Beothuk can't survive

English settlers arrived in Newfoundland in the early 17th century (above). The Beothuk moved inland, away from the sea which was a source of food. They clashed with the Europeans, and their numbers began to fall. The last known Beothuk was a woman named Shanawdithit (right). She died in 1829.

LIVING OFF THE LAND AND SEA

☛ **Lifestyle based on the ocean**

☛ **Beothuk have varied diet**

From spring until winter, the Beothuk lived near the coast. They traveled in birchbark canoes with tall, pointed ends and high sides in the middle. From the canoes, the Beothuk used **harpoons** to fish for salmon, seal, and shellfish, such as lobster. As they moved inland in the late fall, they hunted deer and caribou using spears or bows and arrows.

> "They did not dare advance inland beyond the shooting distance of a crossbow."
> *John Day describes Cabot's visit ashore*

Holy Red

The Beothuk may have thought red was a sacred color. Cabot believed they made red dye from the brazil tree. In fact, it later became known that they used deposits of red ocher, or clay, from the ground.

PAINTED PEOPLE

★ **Bright red decorates everything**

The painted red stick found by Cabot's crew was evidence that the Beothuk had been in the area. Later Europeans noted that the Beothuk used red dye to paint their faces, bodies, weapons, and canoes. The dye may have had a religious significance, but it also acted as a natural repellant to keep away biting insects. Although Cabot did not meet any natives, Europeans captured some Beothuk in the 1500s and took them to Europe as slaves.

I Love Nature

When Cabot reached Canada's rugged shoreline, he believed he had landed in Asia. He was amazed by a land thick with trees and seas full of fish.

ICY ENTRANCE

★ **No reports of icebergs**

★ **Fog makes navigation difficult**

If the *Matthew* stayed north on its voyage in 1497, it likely met icebergs in the north Atlantic. The Labrador Current flows south along the east coast of Labrador and Newfoundland. In the spring and early summer, it carries ice. As the current meets the warm Gulf Stream, fog forms over the sea. The ice and fog may have forced Cabot to turn southwest.

TOWERING TREES

☛ **Land provides ideal ship-building material**

Cabot was impressed with the quantity and height of the trees he saw on land. John Day wrote that, "They found tall trees of the kind masts are made from, and other smaller trees." This suggests Cabot may have landed in Nova Scotia. Large trees are more abundant there. They include tall, straight fir trees, such as the white pine (left) and the balsam fir.

COD, COD EVERYWHERE

+ Seas teeming with life!

"They assert that the sea there is swarming with fish," wrote the Italian Soncino about Cabot's voyage. Off Newfoundland, the seas were said to be so thick with cod that a person "could walk across their backs." Fishing boats from Europe soon began visiting the region. The North West Atlantic fishery fed much of Europe and North America for centuries.

TRAVEL UPDATE

Grazing land

★ John Cabot's stories of his discoveries suggest that settlers heading for eastern Canada should take some animals. Cabot arrived in springtime and found a green, grassy landscape. After discovering some animal dung, Cabot guessed that farm animals grazed on the land. He described the land as a "country … very rich in grass."

THIS MUST BE ASIA!

★ **Sighting of brazilwood and silk**

Cabot claimed to find brazilwood and silk on his first expedition. He probably wanted to assure King Henry VII that he had landed in Asia. When he found a red painted stick, Cabot assumed that native people had used brazilwood, a tropical tree, for their red dye. In fact, the Beothuk used iron oxide from clay deposits.

Fortune Hunting

By the late 1400s, England was eager to profit from trade with Asia. Spanish and Portuguese explorers were already returning from Asia with ships filled with valuable goods.

SOME PEPPER WITH THAT?

☛ Spices are big business

Fifteenth-century Europeans loved exotic Asian spices. Peppercorns, or "black gold," were so valuable they were used as money. Merchants in the Middle East ran the spice trade and kept prices high. Countries such as Spain, Portugal, and England began looking for ways to reach Asia to buy the spices themselves.

THE RACE HEATS UP

+ Henry VII wants a piece of the action

+ Sends explorer west

When Cabot approached Henry VII before his first expedition, the king was eager to build England's wealth and power. If Cabot made any discoveries on his voyage, the king would receive one fifth of the value of anything Cabot found. More importantly, the king hoped to make a fortune if Cabot found a sea route to Asia. This would help increase the status of the king in the eyes of his subjects—and the world.

JEWELED ISLE

★ **Eastern island promises great wealth**

★ **Cabot seeks riches on second voyage**

Cabot believed that on his first voyage in 1497 he had reached part of Cathay, or China. He thought that Cipango, or Japan, would be just south. In the early 14th century, an Italian traveler named Marco Polo who had traveled to China told stories about the island of Cipango. Europeans, including Cabot, believed the island was full of spices and jewels. When Cabot set sail on his second voyage in 1498, he was determined to find Cipango.

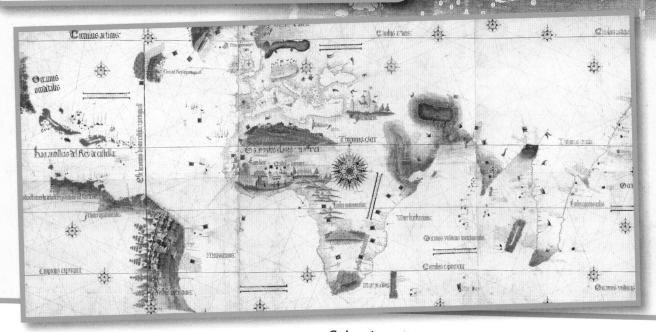

TRICKY TREATY

☛ **Land agreement signed**

☛ **England left out of the deal**

Columbus discovered Hispaniola in the New World in 1492. Spain and Portugal soon began to argue about who could claim these new lands to the west. In 1494, Pope Alexander VI drew up the Treaty of Tordesillas. It divided the New World between Spain and Portugal along an imaginary north–south line (a black vertical line on the left of the map, above). Spain claimed new lands to the west of the line, while Portugal claimed new lands to the east. When Cabot set out to explore for England, he had to be careful not to stray into Spanish or Portuguese territory.

This Isn't What It Said in the Brochure!

John Cabot's successful trip made him famous in his own lifetime. After he disappeared in 1498, the voyages of Christopher Columbus overshadowed Cabot's achievements for centuries.

BETTER LUCK NEXT TIME

★ **First expedition is a failure**

Before he reached Newfoundland, Cabot had already failed in an attempt to launch a voyage in summer 1496. It is not clear what ship he took, but it may have been the *Matthew*. According to John Day, Cabot "had a disagreement with the crew, he was short of food and ran into bad weather." Forced to return to Bristol, Cabot began to make plans for another trip.

MONEY MATTERS

☞ **Relief as Italian bank funds voyage**

Henry VII was happy to give Cabot permission to explore—but not as eager to pay for his voyages. The explorer did not have enough money to pay for the voyage himself, so he had to raise it. He received some funds from wealthy merchants in Bristol (right). In the end, however, most of Cabot's funding came from the Bardi, an Italian banking house in London. At the time, Italian bankers were eager to lend money to promote exploration.

★ **Many explanations exist about Cabot's disappearance. Using the evidence on this page and the following pages, which story do you think is the most likely? Why?**

Did you know?

Cabot's son, Sebastian, was also an explorer. In 1525, Sebastian left Spain and sailed to what are now Argentina and Uruguay. But he did not find the hoped-for passage to the East.

LOST AT SEA?

+ Cabot's final days a mystery

When Cabot set sail in May 1498, one of his ships did not make it very far. It was damaged and returned to Ireland. Perhaps the other ships sank somewhere in the Atlantic, or off Newfoundland. Few people could swim at this time, so the sailors likely drowned. If they did make their way to shore, they may have died from starvation or **hypothermia** from the cold Atlantic waters.

HE'S A DISGRACE!

☞ **Voyagers return empty-handed**

☞ **Cabot in disgrace**

Some historians believe that Cabot did return to England. He may have died soon after his return. The king paid his pension until 1499. If Cabot did return, his reputation would have been in ruins. He had failed to find the route to Asia or any great riches. Cabot did not realize that he had stumbled upon the unknown continent of North America.

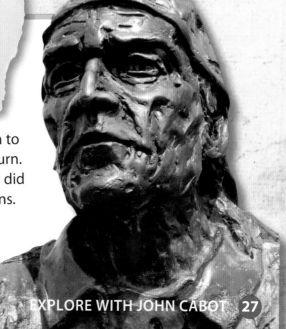

End of the Road

John Cabot did not find the Northwest Passage. He was a hero —then a failure—in his own time. He died not knowing that he had opened the door to European exploration and settlement in North America.

HERO'S RETURN

- ☛ King grants pension and new charter
- ☛ Explorer hailed as a hero

Cabot returned to England in August 1497. King Henry VII must have been pleased with Cabot's achievements. He granted him a reward and a pension, and would support Cabot's next voyage. Cabot became a 15th century celebrity and became known as "The Great Admiral."

THE MISSING LINK?

- ★ Italian relics found

Cabot may have landed in North America a second time in 1498. In 1501, a Portuguese explorer named Gaspar Corte-Real visited Newfoundland. He returned to Europe with 57 Beothuk people. Among their possessions was a pair of silver earrings made in Venice, and an Italian sword. Perhaps Cabot or his men had traded with the Beothuk on the second voyage.

Did you know?

In 1499, the Spanish explorer Alonso de Hojeda said he met Englishmen in what is now Venezuela. Could they have been Cabot and his men? Perhaps the sailors ended up in South America.

FINDINGS SURFACE

★ **Spanish map shows area explored**

Juan de la Cosa was a Spanish navigator who sailed with Columbus. A map drawn in 1500 shows the North American coastline, including the area that Cabot explored. Included on the map are five English royal standards, or flags. A caption states that this area is "sea discovered by the English." This and a map by Sebastian Cabot are the only visual evidence of Cabot's explorations.

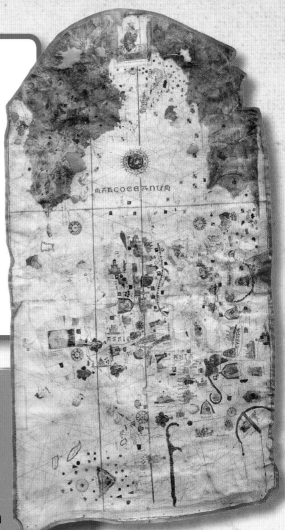

TRAVEL UPDATE

Full sail ahead!

★ Why not cross the Atlantic on the *Matthew*? A replica of the ship was built in 1996 to celebrate the 500th anniversary of Cabot's voyage. The replica uses the same materials that were available in the 15th century. It was also built with the same dimensions as the original. In other words, it's tiny, cramped, and uncomfortable!

CABOT DISAPPEARS

+ **No sign of explorer**

No one knows when or how Cabot died. There are no records of his return to England. According to the Bristol customs office, however, the *Matthew* carried cargo from Bristol to Ireland in 1503. Records also report that the ship departed for Spain in 1504 with another load of goods. If Cabot's ship did return to Bristol, perhaps the explorer died somewhere in North America or on the return voyage home in 1498.

GLOSSARY

Note: Some boldfaced words are defined where they appear in the book.

archaeologists Scientists who study history by digging up old remains

caravels Small, fast sailing ships used by the Spanish and Portuguese in the 15th and 16th centuries

caulked Sealed gaps and seams with waterproof material

compass rose A design showing the directions north, south, east, and west

continental shelf A relatively shallow part of the seabed around the edge of a continent

currents Bodies of water that run in a particular direction

dead reckoning A method of calculating progress at sea by estimating the direction and distance traveled

gimbal A cradle-like device for keeping a compass or other instrument horizontal

harpoons Pointed spearlike weapons attached to ropes that are thrown to hunt sea creatures

hulls The main bodies of ships, including their bottoms, sides, and decks

hypothermia When a person's body temperature drops very low

landfall A place of arrival on land from the sea

latitude The distance of a place north or south of the equator, usually expressed in degrees

letters patent Official documents issued by a ruler to give a subject specific rights, such as the right to explore a particular territory

magnetic field A region that is affected by the force of magnetism

mariner Someone who navigates a ship

navigate To direct the course of a ship or aircraft

New World North and South America

Northwest Passage A sea route that was said to lead to Asia by passing around the top of North America

oakum Loose threads of fiber, usually made by untwisting old ropes

pension A regular payment given to someone who is too old to work

port A city, town, or other place where ships load or unload goods

provisions Supplies for a journey, including food, drink, and equipment

---

Giovanni Caboto is born, probably in Genoa, Italy.

After living in Venice for 15 years, Cabot becomes a Venetian citizen.

While working as a civil engineer in Valencia, Spain, Cabot may have met Christopher Columbus on his return from discovering the New World.

c.1450 **1461** **1476** **1482** **1493** **1495**

Cabot's family moves to Venice, where he becomes a merchant trading with the Middle East.

Cabot marries Mattea; the couple have three sons: Ludovico, Sebastian, and Sancto.

In late 1494 or early 1495, Cabot moves to Bristol, a thriving port in the west of England.

ON THE WEB

www.bbc.co.uk/history/historic_figures/cabot_john.shtml
A biography of Cabot from the BBC history pages.

www.history.com/topics/exploration/john-cabot
History.com page about Cabot, with links to videos about the explorer.

www.rmg.co.uk/explore/sea-and-ships/facts/explorers-and-leaders/john-and-sebastian-cabot
Facts about Cabot and his son Sebastian from Britain's National Maritime Museum.

www.enchantedlearning.com/explorers/page/c/cabot.shtml
A brief biography and timeline of John Cabot from Enchanted Learning.

BOOKS

Doak, Robin. *Cabot: John Cabot and the Journey to North America* (Exploring the World). Compass Point Books, 2003.

Larkin, Tanya. *John Cabot* (Famous Explorers). Powerkids Press, 2003.

Mass, Wendy. *John Cabot: Early Explorer* (Explorers!). Enslow Elementary, 2004.

Rice, Earle Jnr. *John Cabot* (Profiles in American History). Mitchell Lane Publishers, 2006.

Roberts, Steven. *John Cabot* (Junior Graphic Famous Explorers). Powerkids Press, 2013.

Taylor-Butler, Christine. *Explorers of North America* (True Books: American History). Children's Press, 2008.

March: King Henry VII gives Cabot and his three sons the right to explore in the Atlantic.

May: Cabot leaves Bristol on the *Matthew* with a crew of 18 to 20 men.

The king stops paying Cabot's pension. Cabot may therefore have survived the voyage, only to die in 1499.

1496

1497

1498

1499

Summer: Cabot makes a first voyage into the Altantic but soon gives up and returns home.

June 24: Cabot and his men make landfall somewhere in what is now eastern Canada, becoming the first Europeans of the time known to land in North America.

May: Cabot and five ships leave Bristol on a second voyage. One ship returns to Ireland: the other four are never heard from again, although evidence suggests they may have reached North America.

INDEX